SAABHU

THE YORKSHIRE TERRIER

WRITTEN BY: ROSEY KAUR

ILLUSTRATED BY: GURPREET BIRK

Saabhu
Copyright © 2020 by Rosey Kaur

All rights reserved. No part of this publication may be reproduced, distributed, or transmitted in any form or by any means, including photocopying, recording, or other electronic or mechanical methods, without the prior written permission of the author, except in the case of brief quotations embodied in critical reviews and certain other non-commercial uses permitted by copyright law.

tellwell

Tellwell Talent
www.tellwell.ca

ISBN
978-0-2288-4230-9 (Paperback)

This book is dedicated to every animal on this planet.

In Memory of Saab Saha Singh.

May 2006-July 2020

My Mommy brought me a red toy. It was my first toy ever. I called it my Red Chicken best friend. I would play with all the time.

When my Mommy brought me home, she brought me in a green bag. I loved my green bag so much. It made me feel safe and comfortable. I enjoyed going inside it when we travelled everywhere.

My bed was so soft and warm. I would take my naps and dream beautiful things. My Mommy would always tuck me in with my blue blanket and stay close to me.

When I was a baby, my Mommy would rub my belly and make me feel better. I loved it when Mommy would rub it forever and ever.

I love going outside and rolling in the grass. Hearing the birds chirp, the squirrels run up and down the trees made my days very special. My Mommy would let me sit in the sun and enjoy the warmth on my little furry body.

Whenever it was a special day, my Mommy would make me my favourite food. It was white rice with steamed carrots. My birthdays were extra special because she would add in lots of carrots.

My Mommy would always dress me up for Halloween. Every year I would get a new costume. My favourite one was the one I am wearing. Can you guess what I am?

My Mommy would bathe me every night and when I got dirty. I enjoyed my bath time especially when Mommy would sing to me. "Saabhu, Saabhu, I love you. Saabhu, Saabhu, I love you."

Whenever my Mommy would bring home pizza, I would make sure I ran down the stairs and got my favourite part. Can you guess what it was? Yes, you got it right, it was the crust.

My Mommy would always take me with her when she went out. I enjoyed driving with her and sticking my head out the window. We drove all the way to Canada.

This was my first selfie with my Mommy. She always wanted me to be in her pictures. She would always say, "Saabhu, picture. Saabhu, smile." I enjoyed taking pictures with my Mommy.

When I was a baby, I had a favourite white chair that I would always sit on. It was a special chair that I kept close to my heart. Do you have a special chair that you sit on?

My Mommy would pray with me and made sure I remembered God all the time. She would cover my head with a beautiful orange scarf.

I love my Mommy and my Mommy loves me the most.

My Mommy chose me when I was all alone in a kennel. I was very happy to be in her life for fourteen years. I love you Mommy.